TRADITIONS AND CELEBRATIONS

HAJJ

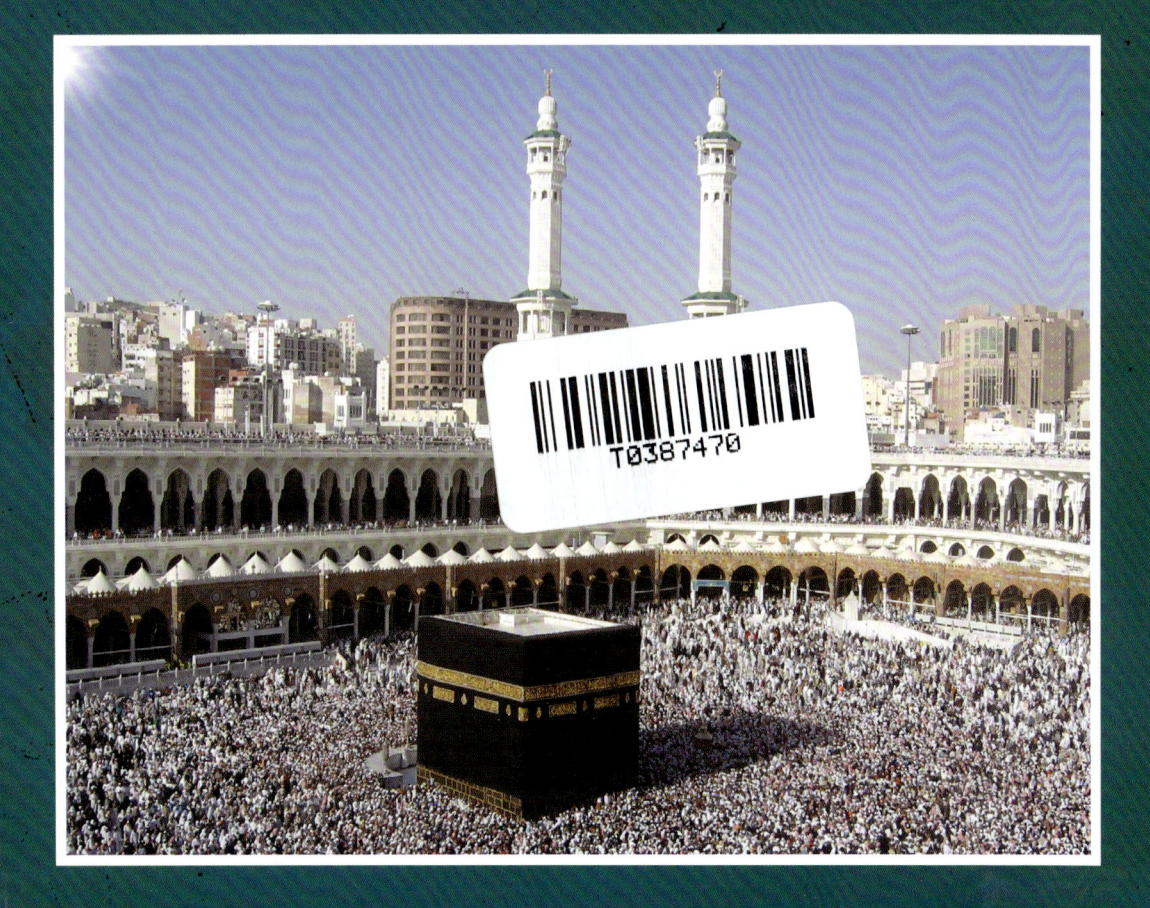

by Golriz Golkar

PEBBLE

a capstone imprint

Published by Pebble, an imprint of Capstone
1710 Roe Crest Drive, North Mankato, Minnesota 56003
capstonepub.com

Library of Congress Cataloging-in-Publication Data is available on the Library of Congress website.

ISBN: 9798875219818 (hardcover)
ISBN: 9798875219764 (paperback)
ISBN: 9798875219771 (ebook PDF)

Summary: Discover how the shared journey of Hajj brings Muslim people together in solemn promises and joyful celebration.

Editorial Credits
Designer: Elijah Blue; Media Researcher: Jo Miller; Production Specialist: Tori Abraham

Image Credits
Getty Images: iStock/hasan zaidi, 29, iStock/Muhammad Nawir, 15; Shutterstock: Aditya E.S. Wicaksono, 13, ahmad.faizal, 23, Andrew V Marcus, 12, as-artmedia, 18, 22, ayazad, 1, diplomedia, 27, ESB Professional, cover, FarisFitrianto, 16, Gatot Adri, 19, Hasan Hatrash, 21, Leo Morgan, 17, lula albab, 26, MAHYUDDIN PAGALA, 10, RBagusdiani, 11, Skill Surface Graphics, 25, Sony Herdiana, 24, Ummi Hassian, 4, wing-wing, 9, ZouZou, 5, Zurijeta, 7

Design Elements
Shutterstock: Rafal Kulik

Printed and bound in China. 006276

TABLE OF CONTENTS

Words in **bold** are in the glossary.

What Is Hajj?

It is a hot day in Mecca, Saudi Arabia. Millions of **Muslims** gather together. These **pilgrims** are on a journey called Hajj. It is an important part of the religion of **Islam**.

Muslims enter the holy area of Mecca.

Pilgrims take part in Hajj in Mecca, Saudi Arabia.

Hajj lasts about five days. Adult Muslims must go at least once in their lives if they are healthy and have enough money to go. Sometimes children go too.

Pilgrims pray at the Kaaba **shrine**. It is the house of Allah, or God. They follow the steps of the Prophet Muhammad. He was the messenger of God. He was born in Mecca. Pilgrims also perform religious **rituals**.

The Kaaba shrine

When Is Hajj?

Muslims follow the **lunar** calendar. It has 354 days. When they see a crescent moon, a new month begins.

The last month of the year is known as Dhul Hijja. Its first ten days are called blessed days in the **Qur'an**. This is the Muslim **holy** book.

Hajj starts on the eighth day of Dhul Hijja. It is a time for getting closer to Allah.

Hajj Begins

Muslims from all over the world travel to Saudi Arabia for Hajj. The Saudi government prepares for them all year long. It makes sure visitors have enough food and housing. It brings buses and cars for travel. It offers guidebooks written in many languages.

Pilgrims arrive at Miqat.

Pilgrims start at an area near Mecca called Miqat. They wash their hands and bodies. They change into light cotton clothes. Wearing similar clothes make them equals before Allah. Then they go to Mecca to begin Hajj.

The First Rituals

The first ritual at Mecca is Tawaf. Its name comes from the Arabic word meaning "to circle around." Pilgrims enter the Holy **Mosque**. They walk around the Kaaba seven times. This stands for the circle of life. Everyone kisses or touches the Kaaba. They pray to Allah.

Everyone performs the Tawaf the same way. It shows they are all equal before Allah. It does not matter who they are or where they come from.

The next ritual is called sa'i.
In Arabic, it means "to walk or run."
It takes place near the Kaaba.

Pilgrims run seven times between
two hills. They remember the story
of the Prophet Ibrahim's wife, Hajar.
Long ago, her baby was dying of
thirst. She ran between the hills to
find water. The angel Jibril appeared.
He dug up the ground. A spring of
water called Zamzam rose up.

Pilgrims start sa'i at one of the hills.

بداية الصفا
SAFA START
شروع صفا

The pilgrims honor Hajar during sa'i. They remember that sometimes it's hard to do good things. Inside the mosque is the Zamzam well. This is where Jibril appeared. People drink this water during Hajj.

A pilgrim drinks Zamzam water.

At night, the pilgrims travel to the nearby town of Mina. They eat light meals of dried fruits and seeds. They sleep in tents.

The Day of Arafat

Pilgrims leave Mina on the second day. They go to the plain of Arafat before sunrise. Muslims believe the Prophet Muhammad gave his last sermon there. He asked Muslims to come together as equals.

Many people **fast**, or avoid eating, on this day. They stand side by side. They ask for good health and wealth. They also ask Allah to forgive and protect them.

At sunset, they go to a nearby camp. They collect stones there for the next ritual.

Return to Mina

Pilgrims return to Mina on the third day. It is the day of Eid al-Adha. This Muslim festival honors the Prophet Ibrahim.

Allah told Ibrahim to **sacrifice** his son. He wanted Ibrahim to prove his faith in Allah. A bad spirit told Ibrahim to ignore Allah. But Ibrahim threw stones at it until it went away. Then Ibrahim agreed to give up his son. But Allah saved the son out of kindness. Ibrahim sacrificed an animal instead.

Pilgrims gather again at Mina.

At Mina, pilgrims throw pebbles at walls. These walls stand for the bad spirit.

Then pilgrims sacrifice a lamb, goat, or other animal. The meat is cut up and cooked. It is shared with poor people. The pilgrims feel grateful. They can help those in need.

Pilgrims stay in Mina for two more days. They throw stones and pray. They wish bad spirits away.

Pilgrims from Malaysia rest at Mina.

Back to Mecca

Pilgrims return to Mecca on the last day of Hajj. They perform Tawaf and sa'i again. Then they change into their normal clothes. Men shave their heads. Women cut off a lock of hair. They all feel like better people. They feel closer to Allah.

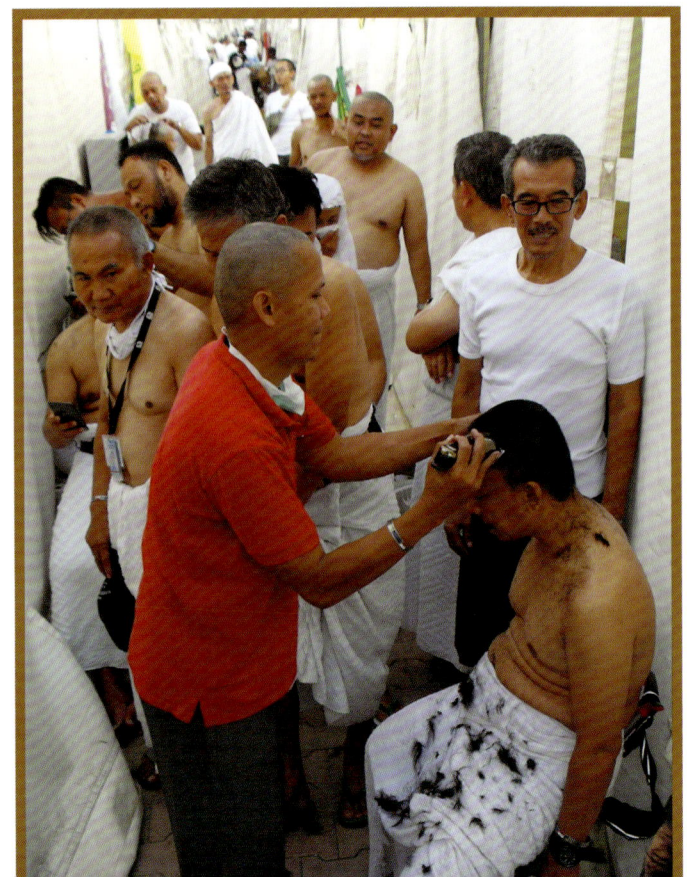

The tomb of the Prophet Muhammad in Medina

Some people return home after Hajj. Others travel to nearby Medina. They may visit the Prophet Muhammad's tomb there.

Many Muslims celebrate Hajj without traveling. They say daily prayers and read the Qur'an at home. They give money and food to poor people. Many fast on the second day.

Muslims around the world celebrate Eid al-Adha. They have large feasts with friends and family.

Many Muslims go on Hajj just once in their lives. Some go many times. Muslims who cannot go may ask someone to go for them.

Hajj is a joyful experience for Muslims. They celebrate Islam. They think of ways to help others. They pray to become better people. Hajj brings them closer to Allah and to each other.

GLOSSARY

fast (FAST)—to avoid eating

holy (HOH-lee)—connected to a god or a religion

Islam (ISS-luhm)—the religion of Muslims, based on the teachings of the Prophet Muhammad communicated to him through the angel Jibril

lunar (LOO-nur)—having to do with the moon

mosque (MOSK)—a place of worship for Muslims

Muslim (MUHZ-luhm)—a follower of the religion of Islam; Muslims believe in one God, Allah, and that Muhammad is his prophet

pilgrim (PILL-gruhm)—a person who travels to holy places to worship

Qur'an (kur-AWN)—a holy book of writings that Muslims believe are the words of Allah

ritual (RIH-choo-uhl)—a series of acts done in a specific way

sacrifice (SAH-kruh-fise)—to offer or give up something valuable; in religion, the offering is to a god

shrine (SHRINE)—a tomb for the dead

READ MORE

Gutta, Razeena Omar. *Zamzam for Everyone: Sharing Water at Hajj*. Concord, MA: Barefoot Books, 2024.

Mohamed, Mariam. *Eid Al-Adha*. North Mankato, MN: Capstone, 2022.

Senker, Cath. *A Muslim Life*. New York: PowerKids Press, 2020.

INTERNET SITES

BBC Bitesize: Introduction to the Early Islamic Civilization
bbc.co.uk/bitesize/articles/zr8m2v4#zjgc4xs

BBC Bitesize: What Is Islam?
bbc.co.uk/bitesize/articles/zrxxgwx

CBC Kids: All about Eid Al-Adha
cbc.ca/kids/articles/learn-all-about-the-muslim-festival
-eid-al-adha

INDEX

ABOUT THE AUTHOR

Golriz Golkar is the author of more than 40 nonfiction books for children. Inspired by her work as an elementary school teacher, she loves to write the kinds of books that students are excited to read. She loves to travel and study languages. Golriz lives in France with her husband and young daughter, Ariane.